Welcome

Woburn Abbey has been home to The Dukes of Bedford for over 300 years but it wasn't until my grandfather, Ian, the Thirteenth Duke, came here following the death of his father in 1953 that it was fully opened to the public. He inherited a house that had fallen into a very poor state of repair during the course of the war and a huge bill for death duties. Rather than hand over the house to The National Trust, he was determined to restore Woburn Abbey to the family home it had always been and stopped at almost nothing to make it a successful enterprise, ensuring the Abbey and its world-famous collection of treasures would be saved for future generations. The collection that you can see now continues to be augmented and enriched by new items, antique and modern, so there is always something new to discover when you visit.

My grandfather left Woburn in 1974, handing over to my parents, Robin and Henrietta, the Marquess and Marchioness of Tavistock, who moved in to the Abbey to continue the amazing job of breathing life back into this wonderful home and Estate.

My father's incredible foresight in creating and establishing Woburn Golf Club successfully brought the game of golf to Woburn with the opening of The Duke's course in 1976. The Club quickly became an established venue in the world of tournament golf and now boasts three championship courses. Together, my parents also re-established the Bloomsbury Stud, whose bloodstock has become famous worldwide, both on the racecourse and at stud. Sadly, my father died suddenly in 2003 shortly after he and my mother had moved out of the Abbey to enjoy their 'retirement'. My mother continues to live on the Estate.

The Abbey itself lies at the heart of an Estate whose activities are many and varied. We have the award-winning Safari Park and The Inn at Woburn, located at the heart of the village – two of the newer threads in the history of the Estate which help support the more traditional activities of farming, forestry and, of particular pride, the outstanding deer herds that you will see roaming freely through the Park.

Although Woburn Abbey is a historic country house, it is also our home. Louise and I – along with our children Alexandra and Henry – are lucky to live in such a beautiful place. We hope that you will enjoy your visit to Woburn.

Andrew Bedford

The West Front of Woburn Abbey

History

BUILDING THE ABBEY

The history of Woburn Abbey begins in 1145. Hugh de Bolebec founded a religious house for a group of Cistercian monks, with the monastic buildings following the usual Cistercian pattern. Thus the present north wing is on the site of the monastic church, while the courtyard marks the great cloister and garth.

In 1538 the Abbot, Robert Hobbes, was found guilty of treason by Henry VIII and the monastery confiscated. Legend says the Abbot was hanged from an oak tree at the Abbey's gate and identifies this as an oak still growing in the Park.

THE RUSSELL FAMILY

The first ancestor whom we can identify with certainty is Stephen Russell of Dorset, who in 1394 represented Weymouth in Parliament. His great-great-grandson John established the family fortune. Having entered the service of Henry VII he later enjoyed the privileged position of a Gentleman of the Privy Chamber, entrusted with many state offices and diplomatic missions under Henry VIII. Most of the family estates were granted in recognition of his services and he became Baron Russell. Henry died in 1547 but his son, Edward VI, granted Woburn Abbey to John the same year. In 1550, following the instructions in his father's will, he created John the first Earl of Bedford.

LEFT John, First Earl of Bedford, after Hans Holbein.

However, Woburn Abbey did not become a family home until 1619 when the childless Third Earl relinquished Woburn to his cousin and heir, Francis, Lord Russell, later Fourth Earl. The latter established it as the principal family seat, building a two-storey wing on the north side, including the fantastic Grotto chamber in the centre of the ground floor. The Earl's improvements were almost certainly the work of Nicholas Stone, the King's future Master Mason. It is through this wing that you enter the Abbey today.

Social enterprises were carried out by the family, such as the draining of the Fens by the Fourth Earl, to reclaim tens of thousands of acres of very fertile agricultural land. During the English Civil Wars the Earl's sons and sons-in-law chose differing sides. The future Fifth Earl at first became General of the Horse for Parliament but changed sides after becoming disillusioned with the latter's politics. Charles I's third visit to Woburn Abbey was as a prisoner in 1647, when he was interviewed here by Oliver Cromwell.

Other Russells became prominent in Parliament, most notably the Fifth Earl's son, William, Lord Russell, leader of the Whigs in the Commons during the Protestant Succession Crisis in the reign of Charles II. His wrongful execution in 1683 for his alleged role in the Rye House Plot to assassinate the King led to a complete posthumous pardon by William III in 1694, which also gained for his father the title of Duke of Bedford and later Marquess of Tavistock, in recognition of the family's sacrifice in this cause.

The Russells have also distinguished themselves in other spheres of public service; as ambassador to France the Fourth Duke negotiated in 1763 the Treaty of Paris, which ended the Seven Years' War.

TIMELINE

1145 Hugh de Bolebec founds Woburn Abbey, with monks from Fountains Abbey

1506 John Russell taken into service by Henry VII

1526 Chenies Manor brought into the family by marriage of Ann Sapcote to Sir John Russell

1538 Abbot Robert Hobbes executed for treason by Henry VIII and Woburn Abbey dissolved

1547 Sir John Russell given Woburn, Tavistock and Thorney abbeys

1550 Sir John created 1st Earl of Bedford

1552 Covent Garden and Long Acre given to 1st Earl following the attainder of the Duke of Somerset

1572 State visit by Elizabeth I to Francis, 2nd Earl, at Woburn Abbey

1100 1150 1150 to 1500 1500 1510 1520 1530 1540 1550 1560 1570

1ST EARL   2ND EARL

RIGHT Plan of Abbey 1661.
BELOW *View of Covent Garden Market,* by Pieter Angillis, *c.*1726.
BOTTOM LEFT The Grotto.

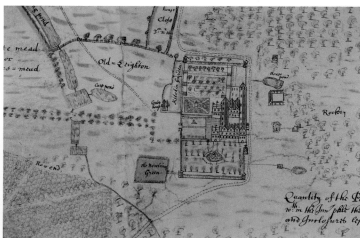

LEFT Rachel Wriothesley, wife of William, Lord Russell; studio of Sir Peter Lely. ABOVE William the Martyr, son of Fifth Earl and First Duke, by John Riley, and (RIGHT) the pamphlet on his trial.

1631
Francis develops estates at Covent Garden, designed by Inigo Jones

1630s
Francis builds two-storey north wing, with grotto (Nicholas Stone and Isaac de Caus)

1619
Francis, 4th Earl, moves family into Abbey

1636
State visit by Charles I and Henrietta Maria

1645
State visit by Charles I

1647
Charles I brought to Woburn under guard, interviewed by Cromwell and Ireton

1669
Bloomsbury estates brought into the family by marriage of Rachel Wriothesley to William, Lord Russell

1683
Execution of William, Lord Russell, for involvement in Rye House Plot

1694
Pardon issued and Earldom elevated to Dukedom. Creation of the title 'Marquess of Tavistock'

1590	1600	1610	1620	1630	1640	1650	1660	1670	1680	1690	1700

3RD EARL	4TH EARL	5TH EARL AND 1ST DUKE

REBUILDING THE ABBEY

In 1747, the Fourth Duke commissioned Henry Flitcroft to rebuild the west wing, including the grand series of state rooms, turning the Abbey into the graceful Palladian house that we see today. The Fifth Duke came of age in 1786 and chose Henry Holland to work at Woburn. Today, there remain his Chinese Dairy, Sculpture Gallery and the south wing containing the Dining Room and Library.

The Sixth Duke, who succeeded his brother in 1802, employed Jeffry Wyatt to design the flower houses and Humphry Repton to landscape the park as it appears today.

Nine species of deer roam freely, including the Milu (commonly known as the Père David) from China, saved from extinction by Herbrand, the Eleventh Duke.

TOP The Chinese Dairy today and from Repton's 'Red Book'.
RIGHT Red deer stags in the 3,000-acre deer park.

ABOVE The London entrance.
ABOVE RIGHT John, the Fourth Duke, by Sir Joshua Reynolds.
ABOVE FAR RIGHT The Sculpture Gallery.

1789–1790
Holland builds the Conservatory (the Sculpture Gallery)

1787
Francis, 5th Duke, employs Henry Holland to rebuild the south wing plus the Indoor Riding School and Tennis Court, and Chinese Dairy

1747–1761
John, 4th Duke, employs Henry Flitcroft to rebuild the Abbey west wing, including the state rooms

1710	1720	1730	1740	1750	1760	1770	1780	1790

2ND DUKE	3RD DUKE	4TH DUKE	5TH DUKE

LEFT *Woburn Sheepshearing*, 1804, by George Garrard.

BELOW LEFT AND BELOW Present and proposed approaches to the house, from Humphry Repton's *Red Book for Woburn Abbey*, 1804.

ABOVE *The Children's Cottage and Garden*, from Humphry Repton's *Red Book for Endsleigh*, 1814.

ABOVE John, Sixth Duke, by Sir George Hayter.

FAMILY ACHIEVEMENTS

Lord John Russell, brother of the Seventh Duke, carried the first great electoral reform bill through Parliament in 1832 and twice became Prime Minister to Queen Victoria.

Several nineteenth-century family members entered the diplomatic service and army.

The Eleventh Duke, a military man, played a constant and unostentatious part in the business of the House of Lords, though his great interest in animals and natural history ensured that he was never more content than during his 37-year presidency of the Royal Zoological Society.

1802
John, 6th Duke, employs Jeffry Wyatt to design the flower houses

1805
Humphry Repton's Red Book of Woburn

1812
Wyatt builds Endsleigh, near Tavistock

1832
Lord John Russell, brother of 7th Duke, passes Reform Bill through Parliament

1841
Queen Victoria and Prince Albert visit Woburn Abbey

1872–1891
Hastings, 9th Duke, contributes to agricultural experiments, school improvements and tenant welfare

1903
Model cottage hospital opened in Woburn village

1800　1810　1820　1830　1840　1850　1860　1870　1880　1890　1900

| 6TH DUKE | 7TH DUKE | 8TH DUKE | 9TH DUKE | 11TH DUKE |

10TH DUKE

WAR AND RECOVERY

On the outbreak of the First World War in 1914, the Eleventh Duke and Duchess turned both the Cottage Hospital in Woburn village, and the Indoor Riding School and Tennis Court in the Abbey grounds, into military hospitals. Duchess Mary took on the punishing role not only of administrator but also of nurse.

During the Second World War, the house and grounds were used for the dissembling of black propaganda and for the billeting of Wrens working at the code-breaking centre at nearby Bletchley Park. The park was used as a satellite airfield.

The aerial view (right) shows the Abbey as it was before the east wing and the great Indoor Riding School and Tennis Court, also designed by Henry Holland, were demolished in 1949–1950. They were irretrievably infected with dry rot. Sir Albert Richardson sealed off the truncated walls of the house and designed the flank walls and the ornamental balustrade now marking the site of the east wing.

My grandfather, the Thirteenth Duke, faced with huge death duties, decided to keep up the family home rather than give it to the National Trust and, to help finance it, opened the house to the public in 1955. Woburn Abbey was one of the first to do so, at a time when there was little competition from other great houses, theme parks, computer games or shopping centres! The house was open all year round and crowds queued to see its treasures and perhaps catch a glimpse of the Duke or Duchess, who had a keen eye for opportunities to publicise the attraction. In 1970 he opened Woburn Safari Park, the second of its kind in Britain.

In 1974 the Duke and Duchess moved abroad and left the Estate in the capable hands of my father, Robin, Marquess of Tavistock. His great legacy was the creation of the three international golf courses and, together with my mother, Henrietta, they became television favourites via the ever-popular series 'Country House'. His tragic death in June 2003 after only eight months as Duke meant the helm passed into my hands as Fifteenth Duke of Bedford.

Today at Woburn we share with our visitors the many beautiful objects that my ancestors collected as patrons of the arts.

ABOVE LEFT Mary, Duchess of Bedford, in her nurse's uniform. **TOP** Aerial view of the Abbey before 1949. **ABOVE** The Indoor Riding School and Tennis Court, demolished 1949/50.

1914
Mary takes on the role of nurse at the military hospital

Indoor Riding School and Tennis Court turned into military hospital by Mary, wife of 11th Duke

1918
Covent Garden estate sold

1926
Mary takes up flying

1920
Abbey Hospital closed

1929
Record flight to India in four days

1930
Record flight to the Cape

1937
Mary disappears on solo flight

1939–1945
Woburn estates taken over for black propaganda, billeting of Wrens from Bletchley Park and as a satellite landing ground

1949–1950
East wing, together with Indoor Riding School and Tennis Court, are demolished

1955
The Abbey opens to public visitors

1920 — 1930 — 1940 — 1950 — 1960

11TH DUKE — 12TH DUKE

ABOVE The Safari Park opened in 1970.
RIGHT Robin, Marquess of Tavistock
and Henrietta, Marchioness.
FAR RIGHT The Marquess' Course,
3rd hole.

1974
Robin, Marquess of
Tavistock, takes over the
running of the Estate

1976
First golf course,
'The Duke's',
opens at Woburn

2003
The Fourteenth Duke dies in June,
Andrew the Fifteenth and present
Duke inherits the Estate

1970
The Thirteenth
Duke opens
Woburn
Safari Park

1978
Second golf course,
'The Duchess',
opens at Woburn

2000
Third golf course, 'The
Marquess', opens at Woburn

2005
Henry born, son of
the Fifteenth Duke

1970   1980   1990   2000   2010

13TH DUKE   15TH DUKE

14TH
DUKE

Family Tree

John, First Earl

Francis, Second Earl

Edward, Third Earl

Francis, Fourth Earl

William, Fifth Earl and First Duke

Wriothesley, Second Duke

Wriothesley, Third Duke

John, Fourth Duke

Francis, Fifth Duke

John, Sixth Duke

Henry Russell (d. 1463) = Elizabeth Herring

John Russell (d. 1505) = Alice Froxmere

James Russell (d. 1509) = Alice Wyse

John, First Earl of Bedford (d. 1555) = Anne Sapcote

Francis, Second Earl (1527–1585) = Margaret St John

Francis (d. 1585) = Juliana Foster   William (d. 1613) = Elizabeth Long

Edward, Third Earl (1572–1627) = Lucy Harington

Francis, Fourth Earl (1593–1641) = Katherine Bridges

William, Fifth Earl and First Duke (1616–1700) = Lady Anne Carr

William, Lord Russell (1639, executed 1683) = Lady Rachel Wriothesley,
daughter of Earl of Southampton

Wriothesley, Second Duke (1680–1711) = Elizabeth Howland

Wriothesley, Third Duke (1708–1732) = Lady Anne Egerton,
daughter of Duke of Bridgewater

John, Fourth Duke (1710–1771) = 1. Lady Diana Spencer (d. 1735)
2. Gertrude Leveson-Gower

Francis (1739–1767) = Lady Elizabeth Keppel, daughter of Earl of Albemarle

Francis, Fifth Duke (1765–1802)

John, Sixth Duke (1766–1839) = 1. Hon. Georgiana Byng (d. 1801)
2. Lady Georgiana Gordon, ten children

Continued opposite

Francis, Seventh Duke

William, Eighth Duke

Continued from previous page

(John, Sixth Duke)

Francis, Seventh Duke (1788–1861) = Lady Anna Maria Stanhope

Lord William (1790–1846)
= Elizabeth Rawdon,
granddaughter of Earl of Moira

William, Eighth Duke (1809–1872)

Lord John (1792–1878)

Hastings, Ninth Duke

Sackville, Tenth Duke

Hastings, Ninth Duke (1819–1891) = Lady Elizabeth Sackville-West

Sackville, Tenth Duke (1852–1893) = Lady Adeline Somers

Herbrand, Eleventh Duke

Hastings, Twelfth Duke

Herbrand, Eleventh Duke (1858–1940) = Mary Tribe

Hastings, Twelfth Duke (1888–1953) = Louisa Whitwell

John, Thirteenth Duke

John, Thirteenth Duke (1917–2002) = 1. Clare Hollway (d. 1945)
2. Lydia Yarde-Buller (d. 2006)
3. Nicole Milinaire

Francis (b. 1950) = 1. Faith Carrington (née Ibrahim)
2. Sarah Clemence

Czarina (b. 1976)

John (b. 1997)   Harry (b. 1999)

Robin, Fourteenth Duke

Robin, Fourteenth Duke (1940–2003) = Henrietta Tiarks (b. 1940)

Rudolf (b. 1944)

Andrew, Fifteenth Duke (b. 1962) = Louise Crammond (b. 1962)

James   = Dawn Alexander
(b. 1975)   (b. 1975)

Robin (b. 1963) = Stephanie Niklas
(b. 1968)

Andrew, Fifteenth Duke

Alexandra (b. 2001)   Henry (b. 2005)

The Book Room

This room formed part of the family quarters until the end of the 18th century but now houses a number of the Library's fine collection of natural history books. It was redecorated in 1976 with wallpaper from a design by Pugin, though the ceiling dates from the mid-18th century.

The metamorphic library table, which forms a set of steps, is by the London maker Mayhew & Ince and cost the Fifth Duke sixteen guineas in 1791. The Sixth Duke, a serious book collector, probably acquired the volumes in the Cabinet du Roy and the works of Pierre-Joseph Redouté. Perhaps the most beautiful book is *Birds of America* by John James Audubon, who spent eighteen years painting more than 1,000 species.

Other items include *L'Antiquité Des Tems Rétablie et Défenduë Contre Les Juifs & les Nouveaux Chronologistes*, 1687, with a 1703 bookplate of Wriothesley, Second Duke: found in the deserted tent of a Confederate soldier during the American Civil War, it was returned to the Ninth Duke by the poet Robert Browning. One of Gillray's political cartoons shows the Fifth Duke (the 'Bedford Bull') pursued by the Duchess of Gordon on behalf of her daughter, Georgiana. When a young girl, the Duchess had ridden down Edinburgh High Street on a pig for a bet. Not surprisingly, some thought her daughter would make an unsuitable match!

In a case opposite the fireplace is displayed the Visitors' Book of 1874, when members of the public could apply by letter for free admission to the house.

Notice the hanging lamp whose central urn once held colza oil to feed the six burners.

FACING PAGE The West Front. **LEFT** John Gould's family of toucans. **ABOVE** Decorative red Morocco binding on *Ordenanzas de Su Magestad para el Govierno Militar de su Armada Naval*, Madrid, 1748. **BOTTOM LEFT** Page from a book of paintings on fungi by Mary (wife of the Eleventh Duke). **BELOW** The Book Room.

The Fourth Duke's Bedroom

The family rooms on the north side included the Fourth Duke's bedroom, placed here partly because he suffered from gout, but also because his newly built state rooms occupied the west wing. The tapestries that originally hung in the family parlour (now the public entrance) dominate this room and were noted here by Horace Walpole in 1751 on his tour of England. They were woven for the Fifth Earl at the Mortlake factory between 1661 and 1664; the shield mark of the factory is visible on the borders and the family coat-of-arms is incorporated at the top of each tapestry. The tapestries are based on cartoons, *The Acts of the Apostles*, painted by Raphael in 1515 for Pope Leo X, who commissioned them for the Sistine Chapel. The original cartoons are owned by the Crown, being on permanent loan to the Victoria and Albert Museum.

On the right as you leave is a marble group by Laurent Delvaux (1696–1778), a Belgian sculptor. The story is from Ovid: Hermaphroditus is seen struggling against the embrace of the water nymph Salmacis. As he rejects her, she prays to the gods that their bodies be united forever. Her wish was granted.

BELOW *The death of Ananias*, and **RIGHT** *The miraculous draught of fishes*, details from the Mortlake tapestries.
FAR RIGHT John, the Fourth Duke, by Thomas Gainsborough.
FACING PAGE The Fourth Duke's Bedroom.

Paternoster Row

The corridor known as Paternoster Row (from the prayer 'Our Father') was built over part of the cloisters of the 12th-century Cistercian monastery. On the left wall are two sketches showing how the monastery and early 17th-century house may have appeared.

The display cases contain family mementoes. In a centre case is a wooden box of toys from Queen Anne's time, discovered in a Bloomsbury Square house in 1931. Also displayed are Lord George William Russell's medals and a scarlet sash that shows the bullet hole from the wound he sustained at the Battle of Talavera (1809) during the Peninsular Campaign.

TOP RIGHT Brass model of gun and carriage, 19th century. **RIGHT** Edward Russell, Admiral of the Fleet, later Earl of Orford, after Sir Godfrey Kneller. **FAR RIGHT** Wriothesley, Second Duke, aged five, in Roman centurion costume, by Sir Godfrey Kneller. **BELOW** Paternoster Row looking towards the Grand Staircase.

RIGHT Walking stick given to William, Fifth Earl, by King Charles I at Woburn in 1647.

The Grand Staircase

Henry Flitcroft designed the Grand Staircase that ascends to the top of the house. There are no visible signs of support, each step being supported and held by the one above and the one beneath. The staircase narrows as it rises from the first floor, giving an impression of even greater height. It is set in a corner of the house rather than centrally, possibly because an earlier staircase had stood nearby.

Flitcroft, the architect who designed the London churches of St Giles-in-the-Fields and St John in Hampstead, played a major role in the rebuilding of Woburn Abbey during the 18th century. When admiring his work all around the Abbey and its grounds it seems inconceivable that some of Flitcroft's contemporaries considered him to suffer 'a lack of creative ability'.

ABOVE John, First Earl, English School, 1555.
ABOVE RIGHT Francis, Second Earl, English School, c.1580. **RIGHT** Italo-Flemish marble group of Atlas and Cupid, 18th century.

On the stairs there is a picture of Chenies Manor in Buckinghamshire, the home of the First Earl of Bedford, who is portrayed on the lower stairs. His granddaughter, Anne, Countess of Warwick, was influential at the court of Queen Elizabeth I. I would also draw your attention to the vibrant portrait of the wife of the Third Earl, Lucy Harington, painted wearing a costume for one of the masques presented by Inigo Jones at Whitehall; she became a close friend of James I's queen, Anne of Denmark, whose portrait you will see in the Long Gallery.

FAR LEFT Francis, Fourth Earl, by Sir Anthony van Dyck.
ABOVE Lucy Harington, c.1610, attributed to John de Critz.
LEFT Detail from a vase, Berlin ware, late 19th century.
FACING PAGE The Grand Staircase.

The Dukes' Corridor

As the name implies, portraits of some of the dukes are displayed here. The dukedom was bestowed on the Fifth Earl in 1694 – you may have noticed his portrait on the staircase landing. Three pairs of brothers have succeeded to the dukedom: the Third and Fourth, Fifth and Sixth and Tenth and Eleventh dukes. John, the Fourth Duke was not well liked, while his Duchess, Gertrude Leveson-Gower, was thought overbearing; yet they provided a loving family home. At the far end, Annigoni's startlingly different portrait of Louisa, wife of the Twelfth Duke, was deliberately requested by her as a joke in order to stand out; I think you will agree that she achieved her aim.

On the window sills are portrait busts of the 19th-century members of the family. In the third window is the bust of Lord John Russell, son of the Sixth Duke. Hanging beside it is his portrait as Prime Minister in the time of Queen Victoria, depicting him holding the Reform Bill of 1832.

LEFT Francis, Marquess of Tavistock, by Sir Joshua Reynolds, c.1765–1766.
BELOW LEFT Hastings, Twelfth Duke, by John Townsend.
BELOW John, Thirteenth Duke, by A. Ropert.

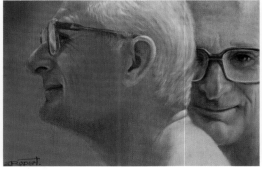

LEFT Robin, Fourteenth Duke, by Richard Stone.
ABOVE The Dukes' Corridor.

The Chinese Room

During the 18th century it was extremely fashionable to have a chinoiserie room in which all the pieces of oriental porcelain could be displayed. In the 19th century this was a guest bedroom; until the end of the Second World War it was called the Venetian Room, probably because of its Venetian window.

The mid-18th century wallpaper, designed for the export market, was brought from China with some of the porcelain on an East Indiaman, possibly the *Tavistock* or the *Streatham*, built by the First and Second Dukes at Rotherhithe.

Extra shapes were also purchased to embellish the already 'busy' wallpaper. The colours have hardly faded since the panels were hung, confirming the excellence of the natural vegetable dyes used.

RIGHT Japanese ivory box carved with rats, Meiji period, late 19th century**.**

You will notice that there is a continuous river landscape flowing around the room, and the plants, trees and birds can be easily identified. This accuracy and attention to detail deeply impressed the great botanist Sir Joseph Banks, a friend of the Fifth Duke.

The ferocious-looking Buddhist lions – the dogs of Fo – standing on the carpet were placed outside houses to prevent evil spirits from entering. The black coffer by the fireplace was made in England in the early 18th century and painted, or 'japanned', to simulate Japanese lacquer.

ABOVE Detail from one of a pair of famille verte dishes, Chinese, Kangxi (1662–1722).
LEFT The Chinese Room.
BELOW Detail of a peacock from the Chinese wallpaper, mid-18th century.

The Flying Duchess' Room

Although remembered as the Flying Duchess, this was only part of the active life of my great-great-grandmother, Mary, wife of the Eleventh Duke. After being educated in England she went to India, where she met her husband, then aide-de-camp to the Viceroy, the Marquess of Dufferin and Ava. They married in India but shortly afterwards, following the death of the Tenth Duke, returned to Woburn as Duke and Duchess.

Mary's love of animals may be seen in the animal portraits. She travelled widely, at times using her yacht, *Sapphire*, for birdwatching expeditions. An example of her photography and the mysterious 'experiment' are to the right of the exit door.

In Woburn she was responsible for establishing a cottage hospital, Marylands, which was a model of its kind. In the First World War she organised temporary wards for wounded soldiers at the Abbey, where she devoted many hours to their care and became a fully qualified theatre sister and radiographer.

In 1925, her great interest in flying developed when she engaged a private pilot and took lessons. In June 1928, Mary accompanied her first pilot, Captain Barnard, on his attempt to break the record to India.

This had to be abandoned, but was successful the following year. A record flight to the Cape followed in 1930, taking 175 flying hours. Other trips were not without incident: these included a forced landing in the Sahara and being shot at by Berber tribesmen in North Africa.

In March 1937, Mary took off in her de Havilland Gipsy Moth aircraft on a short flight to view the flooded Fens and complete her 200 hours of solo flying. By teatime she had not returned and an immediate search, organised by my great-great-grandfather, failed to find her. Some parts of her aircraft were eventually washed ashore near Great Yarmouth, Norfolk.

ABOVE Duchess Mary in her Moth biplane.
RIGHT Mary with Herbrand during one of their walks.
FAR RIGHT *A Charm of Goldfinches among Thistles*, by Archibald Thorburn, 1905.

TOP RIGHT A model of the Duchess' aeroplane.
ABOVE A portrait of Mary, by Lady Abercromby.

BELOW The operating theatre in the Hospital.
BOTTOM Muff, by Joshua Phillimore, a member of the household staff, 1871.

TOP The Flying Duchess' Room.
LEFT The desk used by the Duchess.
ABOVE The Duchess' yacht, *Sapphire II*, by L. Papaluca, *c.*1913.

The Yellow Drawing Room

During the Royal visit in 1841 the Yellow Drawing Room was used by Prince Albert as his sitting room. Prior to this, it had been the French Bedroom, which was redesigned for the Fourth Duke in the latter part of the 1760s after his return from Paris, where he had served as British Ambassador. French influence can also be seen in the single-leaf doors designed to imitate the double doors popular there.

Much of the French furniture you see would have been acquired by him during his stay in Paris. The commode on the left is stamped 'F.M.' for François Mondon, a cabinet-maker working 1736–1770; it was completely restored for us by the furniture department of the Victoria and Albert Museum in a three-year project. The serpentine and *bombé* commode opposite was made in London by the French *émigré*, Pierre Langlois (d. 1767), and cost £78 in 1760.

The portraits feature my 17th-century ancestors. On the left is a fine full-length portrait of William, later the Fifth Earl, with his companion. It was painted in 1627 by the Hungarian artist, Johann Priwitzer, who was commissioned to paint all the Fourth Earl's children. You will see one of my favourites, little Diana with her tame blackbird, in the Long Gallery later. As you leave this room, you will notice a small portrait by Claude Lefèvre (1633–1675) of William Lord Russell, heir to the Fifth Earl, who was executed for high treason in 1683 for his supposed involvement in the Rye House Plot. His executioner was John Ketch, notorious for his blunt instruments.

Over the *bombé* commode is a large painting which depicts Lord Russell's farewell to his wife Rachel and his children on the eve of his execution, painted by John Downman (*c*.1750–1824).

ABOVE Lady Diana and Lady Anne Russell, attributed to John Hayles.
BELOW The Yellow Drawing Room.

The Racing Room

The Racing Room and the Yellow Drawing Room were redecorated, except for the ceilings, in 1993. The wallpaper in both rooms is by Zoffany and is copied from a design called 'Long Gallery' (c.1827), which was found under some boards in Temple Newsam, near Leeds; you will have noticed the same design on the staircase. The ceiling in the Racing Room was probably designed for Henry Flitcroft by the Italian artist, Gianbattista Borra. The room formed part of Prince Albert's suite in 1841 and was furnished for him as a dressing room.

The ceiling was restored in the 1970s after it partially collapsed due to water damage, and the room was refurnished as the Racing Room by my mother. The Bedford colours are still used today by our Bloomsbury Stud, and a copy of the silks can be seen on the chair by the desk.

The neo-classical commodes on either side of the fireplace are also attributed to Pierre Langlois, made for the Marquess of Tavistock c.1760.

The Queen's Gold Cup was won at Ascot by Charles Greville's horse, 'Alarm'; it was presented to the Seventh Duke of Bedford in 1847.

ABOVE The Racing Room.
LEFT The Ascot Gold Cup, by Robert Garrard, 1846.

Queen Victoria's Bedroom

You are now entering the State Apartments. These rooms were kept mainly for visiting royalty and the rest of the time they were shuttered and the furnishings put under chamois or holland covers. Consequently everything remained in excellent condition.

When the house was opened to the public by my grandfather in the 1950s it was accessible every day of the year and we did not have ultraviolet filters on the windows as we do today. Unfortunately, sunlight is a great destroyer of fabric and the wall hangings had to be renewed in 1973, but they are an exact copy of the previous silk of 1820.

Queen Elizabeth I stayed at Woburn during one of her tours in the time of the Second Earl, whilst the house was still in the form of a monastery. Charles I and his Queen stayed in this part of the house in 1636. During the Fourth Duke's rebuilding, the room was gutted and completely redesigned. Now it takes its name from the visit of Queen Victoria and Prince Albert in 1841, when the Royal couple were given this suite of rooms for their use. The Queen wrote in her diary: '… in the bedroom and my dressing-room there are some very fine pictures: in the former hangs one of Lord Russell's trial, by Hayter, one by Wilkie, a Landseer, a beautiful St John by Hayter with his portrait of Lord John and a very fine Eastlake.' All these paintings, with the exception of the Wilkie and the Eastlake, remain in the collection: the recently conserved trial scene still hangs in this bedroom (the large painting in the double-page spread overleaf).

Over the doorways are two portraits by William Fowler of Victoria, one as a young Princess, the other as Queen. The etchings under the trial scene were drawn by Queen Victoria and Prince Albert; these copies were a gift from them to Anna Maria, wife of the Seventh Duke, who had been one of the Queen's ladies-in-waiting.

In the display case is a letter written by the nine-year-old Princess Victoria to Elizabeth Sackville-West, later the wife of the Ninth Duke, on the occasion of her birthday. Also on show are two brooches presented to her when she was one of Victoria and Albert's bridesmaids in 1840.

TOP Princess Victoria, aged nine, by William Fowler. **LEFT** *View on the Coast of Normandy* by Richard Parkes Bonington, c. 1825–1826. **ABOVE** Detail of mirror showing reflection of bed canopy. **FACING PAGE AND OVERLEAF** Queen Victoria's Bedroom.

Queen Victoria's Dressing Room

Prior to Queen Victoria's visit, this room had been furnished and was used as a small drawing room – a room to which one withdrew after rising and dressing or after taking luncheon or dinner.

The room now contains a superb collection of 17th-century Dutch and Flemish paintings, the most notable being two paintings by Aelbert Cuyp (1620–1691): *Nijmegen on the Waal* hangs over the rolltop desk made by Jean Henri Riesener in 1774, and used by Lord John Russell when writing his speeches. Opposite is *Fishermen on the Ice*, a famous winter scene purchased by the Sixth Duke for £1,200 sometime between 1802 and 1806. Over the mantelpiece is a sensitive portrait of Jan Snellinck, a fellow artist, by Sir Anthony van Dyck (1599–1641).

RIGHT *The Hawking Party* by Paulus Potter, 1653.
BELOW *Nijmegen on the Waal* by Aelbert Cuyp.

A favourite of mine is *The Hawking Party*, by Paulus Potter. Over the jib door is a painting by David Teniers (1610–1690), *La Fête aux Chaudrons*, showing the artist (in a red cloak) and his family standing in the left foreground. On the left of the fireplace is a picture of a family party making merry by Jan Steen (1626–1679), entitled *Twelfth Night Feast*. This was acquired by my family around 1754.

The portable firescreens, with panels of blue silk damask to match the wall hangings, were used to protect the ladies' delicate complexions from the heat of the fire.

The elaborately decorated ceilings in these two rooms were designed by Gianbattista Borra and were copied from the remains of a soffit (underside of an arch) discovered in a temple at Palmyra.

There is a beautiful view of the park and Bason Pond from the windows. In the mid-18th century, when the Fourth Duke was First Lord of the Admiralty, a frigate was kept on this pond, which in those days was round. Daniel Defoe mentions it in his *Tour through the Whole Island of Great Britain*, published in 1761:

'...before the House is a very large Bason of Water, surrounded with a fine broad Gravel-walk, which is bounded with Posts and Iron Chains. On the water is a beautiful Yacht, of between 30 and 40 Tons Burden, elegantly carved and gilt, and completely rigged, and mounts 10 Guns, which are fired on Occasion of entertainments given on board her by His Grace.'

ABOVE Queen Victoria's Dressing Room.
LEFT A Louis XVI porphyry vase and cover, c.1803.

The Blue Drawing Room

In the 19th century, afternoon tea was served in this room and Anna Maria, wife of the Seventh Duke, is credited with the 'invention' of this meal. She had found the time between luncheon and dinner too long, so a light tea was served mid-afternoon.

The sofas on either side of the fireplace were made especially for this room. The placing of furniture in an 18th-century room was entirely different from the way we arrange our rooms today. Then, all the chairs would be placed round the walls. Since the wall and chair coverings would often be in the same material, the effect on entering a room could be stunning. Not until the early 19th century did it become fashionable to group furniture in the room.

On the north wall hangs *Landscape with Peasants Dancing* by Claude Lorrain (1600–1682), acquired by the Marquess of Tavistock when in Rome in 1762. One of his letters from London to his friend the Earl of Upper Ossory in 1764 reads: 'I have bought my Claude Lorrain for £220.

It is rather more than it is worth, tho' I have been offered 200 for it – it is a capital picture.'

A blue silk wall-hanging, dating from 1820, used to hang in this room, but it had deteriorated so much over the years that it was decided to replace it with paper, an exact copy of the original but a tenth of the cost. As in the other rooms that have been recently redecorated, the walls of this room are panelled. The panelling had been covered with fine hessian, then lined before finally attaching the padding and blue silk. When this was replaced, we followed the same procedure, and it was interesting to see the 19th-century graffiti that had been drawn on the wooden panelling by the interior decorators – or could it have been the children of the Sixth Duke?

The gilded ceiling was carefully vacuumed and brushed and, as the decoration and plasterwork were in such good condition, it was decided to leave it untouched. I particularly admire the four gilt bronze wall-lights in the neo-classical style (*c*.1780), which the Sixth Duke acquired in 1803 from the well-known Parisian marchand mercier, Lignereux.

Before you leave this room, observe the pier glasses behind you. They were designed by Whittle & Norman, the interior designers commissioned by the Fourth Duke in the 1750s. It is hard to imagine that the glass cost more than the frames.

LEFT *Bureau plat* (writing table), book case and cabinet, *c*.1770 by Phillipe Claude Montigny. **BELOW** Portrait of Daniel Mytens and wife, by Sir Anthony van Dyck.

RIGHT Anna Maria Stanhope as a child, by George Proctor, c.1790.
FAR RIGHT Anna Maria, wife of the Seventh Duke, depicted in a miniature displayed on the Weisweiler cabinet.
BELOW The Blue Drawing Room.

The State Saloon

You are now in the centre of the west wing, with another superb view to the west, and to the east through the double doors into the Long Gallery, which runs along the inside of this wing.

The Saloon rises through the first and second floors, and its coved and coffered ceiling is richly ornamented and gilded. The walls were once hung with blue silk damask, but this became faded and torn. It was carefully removed and preserved for re-upholstering the state furniture, which you will have seen in some of the rooms of this wing. In 1973 my grandfather commissioned Roland Pym to paint the murals which now adorn the Saloon. They illustrate some of the characters and achievements and some of the places which have played an important role in the life of the family. My parents and I were unsure about some of the details in the paintings, such as why my father is shown in glasses with an 18th-century tricorn hat, but our curator, Christopher Gravett, is a medievalist and informs me that glasses first appeared in the late 13th century.

The ingenious folio bookcase with its impressive books, together with the tables and candlestands in the centre of the room, are attributed to Henry Holland. They previously stood for nearly 200 years in the Library.

On the south and north sides are two splendid chimney-pieces of white marble, with their shelves supported by linked terminal figures at the angles, their friezes sculptured with cornucopias in bold relief and a ram's head in the centre. These were carved by the Belgian sculptor, John Michael Rysbrack (1694–1770). The bronze figure of Sir Francis Drake, a godson of the Second Earl, looks wistfully towards the west, perhaps musing on his sea voyages and regretting the disappearance of the Fourth Duke's frigate. This statuette is a reduced version of the large statue of Sir Francis on Plymouth Hoe.

There is a small watercolour by Lady Ela Russell on the left of the exit door, showing the Saloon as it was in 1882. Lady Ela, the elder daughter of the Ninth Duke, painted a number of the Abbey's interiors and of Endsleigh, the cottage orné near Tavistock in Devon built by Wyatville for the Sixth Duke in 1812. Endsleigh appears in the mural on the window wall behind you.

RIGHT The Saloon, c.1920.
BELOW LEFT Detail from the gilt decoration of a shutter.
BELOW Detail showing East India Company from the wall paintings by Roland Pym, commissioned in 1973. **FAR RIGHT** One of a pair of pier glasses, by John West, 1757.
FACING PAGE The State Saloon.

The State Dining Room

One advantage of having the dining room so far from the kitchens was that none of the cooking smells pervaded the family rooms; the domestic offices were in the now-demolished east wing. Nevertheless, food had to be kept warm for the table and this was achieved by the use of covers and stands with burners underneath. They also used dishes with an inner and outer lining, between which hot or cold water was poured as required.

In the 19th century it was the fashion for entrée dishes to be placed on the table while the soup and the fish were eaten. This would be followed by the roasts – saddle of mutton, venison, game, and so on. The puddings would be placed on the table at the same time as the roasts, then all these dishes would be cleared by servants in livery for the service of dessert. This was composed of varieties of fruit, many of which would have been grown on the Estate. At the end of dinner, a signal was given by the hostess and the ladies would rise and leave the room. They would then go back either into the State Saloon or the Blue Drawing Room, where tea would be served. The gentlemen would remain at table with their port and cigars.

At the end of the 18th century and beginning of the 19th, breakfast was served between ten and eleven in the morning, while a few hours later there was a second breakfast (luncheon), which was generally eaten only by the ladies, 'who like to make *la petite bouche* at dinner'.

The delightful dinner service is from the Meissen factory (*c*.1800). It is decorated with a variety of birds and insects, all exquisitely painted. It must have been used frequently since, unfortunately for us today, many pieces are now missing. On the table, there are wine and cordial glasses with air-twist stems (*c*.1760). The flatware is silver gilt, with handles of jasper, agate or bloodstone.

The beautiful Virginian walnut chairs are attributed to Benjamin Goodison (*c*.1740). Notice the crisply carved shells on the knees. They were probably intended as dining chairs, as the same attention has been given to carving the backs as the fronts. Chair backs were usually plain, as they were placed against the walls until the early part of the 19th century. Underneath the side tables are two pairs of mahogany wine coolers, one of which is lead-lined. The ice to cool the bottles came from the ice house in the park.

The gilt bronze wall-lights, decorated with acanthus leaves and berries (*c*.1745), are attributed to Jean-Claude Duplessis, designer and goldsmith to Louis XV.

One of the finest Van Dycks in the collection hangs over the fireplace. It is a portrait of Aubert Lemire, Dean of Antwerp and Almoner and librarian to the Archduke Albert.

LEFT One of a pair of pier glasses, by Whittle and Norman.
BELOW A *seau crenelle* (wine glass cooler) on an oval dish, Meissen, *c*.1800.

LEFT Detail from ceiling decoration by Michael Rysbrack. **RIGHT** Detail from the cornice decoration; the lion was symbolic of Bacchus, god of wine.

TOP AND OVERLEAF The State Dining Room. **LEFT** One of a pair of silver casserole dishes and covers, by W. Burwash and R. Sibley, 1805, on stands with oil burners, by R. Salmon, 1791.

The Breakfast Room

This has been used in the past as a waiting room and a breakfast room, and it is here that we very occasionally have breakfast and where we give informal luncheon and dinner parties.

All the paintings in this room are by the famous 18th-century portrait painter, Sir Joshua Reynolds (1723–1792); one of the most beautiful family portraits in the house is the painting of Lady Elizabeth Keppel in the dress she wore as a bridesmaid at the wedding of Queen Charlotte. In the portrait, she is depicted garlanding the bust of Hymen, the god of marriage.

Elizabeth, daughter of the Earl of Albemarle, was married to Francis, Marquess of Tavistock, only son of the Fourth Duke. Francis, whose portrait hangs near that of his wife, was attractive and intelligent, with a loveable nature. Before his marriage he was popular with the young ladies and it caused some broken hearts, according to Walpole: 'Lord Tavistock has flung his handkerchief and…everybody is pleased that the lot has fallen on Lady Elizabeth Keppel'.

ABOVE The Breakfast Room. **LEFT** Sir Joshua Reynolds, a self-portrait.

BELOW The Marquess of Tavistock in the uniform of the Dunstable Hunt, by Reynolds, c. 1759. **RIGHT** Elizabeth Keppel, Marchioness of Tavistock, by Reynolds, c. 1761.

It proved to be a happy, though tragically short, marriage. Francis died three years later after a hunting accident and Elizabeth, who had been passionately in love with her husband, died 18 months later of a broken heart, leaving three young boys to be brought up by their grandparents.

Some months after the death of her beloved husband, Elizabeth was attended by a physician who was anxious to help her out of decline. Feeling her pulse, he begged Elizabeth to open her clenched hand. With gentle force he overcame her reluctance and saw that she held a miniature of Francis. When he reproached her for hindering her recovery by thus dwelling on her grief, she confessed that the picture had been in her hand or in her bosom ever since the day of her husband's death, and would remain so 'until I drop off after him into the welcoming grave'.

The Duke of Bedford's grief at the loss of his son was no less consuming. Renowned for keeping a daily journal, he left a month of blank pages following the tragedy.

ABOVE Worcester spill vase, c. 1805, painted by William Doe.

The Dining Room

This is the dining room we use when there are more than six of us. It contains the fine collection of Venetian views by Canaletto (1697–1768).

The future Fourth Duke visited Venice while on the Grand Tour in 1731. The paintings were subsequently commissioned and, over the next few years, arrived at Bedford House in London, where they remained until the house was demolished in 1800. The paintings have been here ever since, reminding us of the fascination of this beautiful city for the traveller.

One of our favourites is *The Entrance to the Arsenal* (top left, west wall), where the great fleets of the republic were built, a view largely unaltered since the 18th century.

During the Fourth Duke's time, this room was used as a library. When the south wing was rebuilt between 1787 and 1790, probably by Sir William Chambers, Henry Holland redesigned the interiors and the books were re-housed in the new library.

During the 19th century, the room became known as the Venetian Drawing Room and was hung with green drapery. The room was redecorated recently, and the curtain fabric was chosen to complement the colours in the paintings. We have gone back to an earlier idea in furnishing by covering the dining chairs with loose covers.

From this room, you can see the different levels of the ground between the west and the south. The south terrace was built up over an undercroft to enable the Fifth Duke and his guests to walk out after dinner. The terrace was extended later, and beyond it lie the private gardens with their formal beds and fountains.

ABOVE *View on the Grand Canal with the Bridge of the Rialto.*
ABOVE RIGHT *Entrance to the Grand Canal, with the Dogana and the Church of Santa Maria della Salute.*
RIGHT *The Grand Canal, Ascension Day.*

ABOVE *The Campo Francesco Morosoni from San Stefano.*
ABOVE RIGHT *The Scuola di San Rocco.* RIGHT *View of the*
Doge's Palace at the Piazzetta seen from the Bacino.
BELOW *The Campo Santa Maria Formosa.*
OVERLEAF *The Dining Room.*

The Ante-Library

The Ante-Library has changed little since the 19th century, when it was a map reading room. However, we had to redecorate it in 1993 as the paper lining the walls was deteriorating. The same paint colours were chosen and one or two missing mouldings were replaced, which I hope are not detectable.

Naturally, in all cases of redecoration and conservation, complete records are kept for reference. Over the doors there are grisaille panels depicting cherubs at play. These were designed and painted by Biagio Rebecca (1735–1808) during the latter part of the 18th century, when Henry Holland redesigned the south wing.

RIGHT Cupid ensnared by a mermaid, probably by Sir J.E. Boehm.
BELOW View of the South Front garden through the Ante-Library windows.
BOTTOM The Ante-Library.

The Holland Library

The Holland Library was designed by Henry Holland in the neo-classical style as part of his redevelopment of the south wing in about 1787. It replaced the old library at the south-west corner, which is now the Dining Room. The Holland Library is divided into three parts by screens with fluted Corinthian columns, with the smaller Wood Library beyond. Many of the volumes housed here are concerned with natural history but also geography and history.

TOP The Holland Library. **LEFT** Barometer, a pair with a thermometer, the actions by D. Adams, *c.*1775. **ABOVE** Portrait of a gentleman, by Frans Hals. **ABOVE RIGHT** Portrait of a youth, known as Aelbert Cuyp, circle of Cuyp.

The Armada Portrait

The portrait of Elizabeth I was probably painted by George Gower in 1588. It is known as 'The Armada Portrait' because it commemorates that great victorious sea battle the same year against the Spanish invasion fleet, the latter depicted in the left-hand panel being attacked by English ships and, in the right-hand panel, wrecked by storms around the Scottish and Irish coasts. It is probably the most iconographic portrait of Elizabeth the Virgin Queen, her pure status emphasised by the symbolism both in the colours of her dress and the festoons of highly expensive pearls that she wears. Royal sun-in-splendour badges and jewels decorate her costume, possibly a representation of that worn when the Queen reviewed her troops at Tilbury as the Armada approached. The pink bows seem to be coloured with a purple Persian dye called *ikat*. Unlike other contemporary portraits, this is largely designed as a statement of power and authority. She places her hand firmly on the globe and, to underline her status as Empress of the world, an Imperial crown sits on the table behind her. The mermaid on her chair hints at her command of the seas, aided by her loyal commanders, Drake and Raleigh. The portrait may have been given to Anne, Countess of Warwick, daughter of the Second Earl of Bedford; she had married Ambrose Dudley, brother of the royal favourite, Robert Dudley, and was a courtier and friend of Queen Elizabeth.

The Long Gallery

enry Flitcroft redesigned the Long Gallery in the mid-18th century. During the 16th and 17th centuries it would have been used for exercise and was where the full-length standing portraits would have been hung. Flitcroft changed its structure by turning it into three bays, using Corinthian columns.

During the winter of 1980–1981 the Long Gallery was completely redecorated by our own maintenance team. The old wallpaper was stripped and underneath was discovered the original boarding and scrim. The wallpaper,

by Cole & Son, is hand-blocked and is from a mid-18th century design called 'Pomegranate'.

The bell pulls on either side of the fireplaces were designed and worked by my mother and her friends. The design was copied from some of the carving round the fireplace and the doors, and the border can be seen on the carpet in one of the paintings.

As each bay was completed, the paintings, which had been gathered from other rooms and cleaned, were re-hung. Some had never been on public view before,

LEFT Robert Devereux, Earl of Essex, by Marcus Gheeraedts, 1596.
ABOVE Queen Anna of Denmark, consort of James I, by Marcus Gheeraedts, c.1610–13.
OVERLEAF The Long Gallery.

notably the Priwitzer portraits of the Fourth Earl's children in the middle bay. They have to be carefully monitored as they are painted on panel, like many paintings in the house. If you look closely at the painting of the Long Gallery by Lady Ela Russell (1888) on the easel, you will notice some of these portraits have been returned to the same position.

The window seats in this bay and the north bay, which were found in storage, had suffered badly from woodworm and the ravages of time, so it was decided to have them completely restored and upholstered, as they had been specially designed for this gallery. The upholstery colour was chosen by my mother from the painting of the Fourth Earl as a boy, with his hawk.

The pair of *bureaux encoignures* (corner cupboards) and marriage chests in this bay, in the style of André Charles Boulle, were completely restored in the 1980s. During restoration, it was discovered that the marriage chests had

been made by Thomas Parker *c*.1812 in London, and there is a pair which match these in the Royal Collection.

From the windows, you can see the flight of steps and balustraded retaining wall designed by Sir Albert Richardson in the 1950s. They now cover the area of the east wing, built by Henry Holland in 1790 but pulled down in 1950, together with half of the north and south wings. The northeast corner contained the Great Kitchen. Other domestic offices were housed to the left of the Great Hall, where the steps are now, and on the right were the bedroom suites of my great-great-grandfather, Herbrand, Eleventh Duke, and his elder sister, Ela.

BELOW LEFT Francis, Marquess of Tavistock, by Pompeo Batoni, painted in 1762 whilst on the Grand Tour. **LEFT** Campana vase with classical relief, by Giacommo Zoffoli, late 18th century. **BELOW** Elizabeth Bridges, sister of the Fourth Countess, aged 14, by Hieronimo Custodio, 1589.

Recent Acquisitions

ABOVE Cartoon of Woburn Abbey by J.A.K., captioned: 'I am the Marchioness'.
BELOW Blue John vase on marble plinth, English, c.1780

ABOVE Sèvres mortar from the Bedford gift service, c.1763 which had been missing.

ABOVE Louisa Jane Russell, daughter of John, Sixth Duke of Bedford, by Sir Edwin Landseer. Louisa became Duchess of Abercorn. Here she is dressed as Viola in Shakespeare's Twelfth Night.
RIGHT Toast rack, by Phillip Rundell, London, 1821.
BELOW Goat family, signed bronze by Rembrandt Bugatti, dated 1904. A goat is the crest of the Dukes of Bedford.

The Crypt and Porcelain Displays

At the foot of the crypt stairs are porcelain displays designed by my mother. In the first alcove is the Meissen State Service (*c.*1850), painted with romantic scenes and almost complete. Opposite is a case filled with Wedgwood caneware (1809), used as a picnic service in the Thornery. The middle alcove contains an eye-catching display of 17th-century Japanese porcelain. Some of the pieces, decorated with a quail and millet motif, are Kakiemon, the name of a family of potters from Arita.

A case of English porcelain contains a fine pot pourri vase in the shape of a dovecote from the Chelsea factory (*c.*1755). In the third alcove the fruit plates on the back wall were made at Davenport in 1845 and were used by one of my ancestors in his conservatory; when a guest selected a piece of fruit it was presented on the appropriate plate.

As you enter the Sèvres Room, in the first cabinet on your left is displayed a selection of porcelain from the Sèvres Gift Service. Louis XV presented this service to the wife of the Fourth Duke in appreciation of her husband's role in negotiating the Treaty of Paris in 1763. The pavilion in the centre contains another dinner and dessert service called *rose et feuillage*. It is a mixture of original pieces from the Sèvres factory and copies from other French and English factories. The white figures in the centre are called 'biscuit', unglazed porcelain that is fired only once. Some of the figures are modelled on drawings by François Boucher (1703–1770).

TOP Imari saucer dish painted with crane, Japanese, Edo period, late 17th/early 18th century.
RIGHT Cruet stand from the Wedgwood caneware service, 1809.

LEFT Kakiemon-style dragon wall vase, Japanese, Edo period, late 17th century.
FACING PAGE The Pavilion.

ABOVE Sèvres biscuit group of Croydon and Lisette (*Les Mangeurs de raisins*), modelled by Falconet after Boucher.
RIGHT Dovecot vase, Chelsea, *c.*1755.

ABOVE Vase-à-oignon, Sèvres, 1763, the painting by Dodin.
RIGHT Ewer shaped like a monkey by J.J. Kändler, Meissen, *c.*1738–1740.

The Silver and Gold Vaults

A selection of some of the family silver and gold is displayed in these vaults. The Fourth Duke commissioned Paul de Lamerie, one of the finest Huguenot silversmiths, to make the breadbaskets displayed in cabinet 2 as a wedding present to his second wife, Gertrude.

There is a set of candlesticks by David Willaume, another Huguenot, who lived less than four miles (6.5 km) away in the small village of Tingrith.

In the past some of the family's old outdated silver was melted down and recycled into more fashionable wares, such as the elegant and simple travelling services by John Scofield, or the vigorous Regency splendour of Paul Storr's work, much admired by the Sixth Duke.

Some of the items are used by the family today, in particular the set of 12 individual silver gilt teapots displayed in the gold vaults. These are removed when we have guests, for their morning tea.

Before you leave the vaults do take time to look at the dressing case, a wedding present to Ermyntrude, the Ninth Duke's youngest daughter.

LEFT The Reform Cup by J. & J. Angell, 1832.
BELOW Inscribed bracelet given to Anna Maria, wife of the future Seventh Duke, by Queen Victoria in 1838.

RIGHT Silver figure based on 18th-century paintings of the Bedfordshire Militia, commissioned by the Eleventh Duke in 1895.
LEFT The decorative silver gilt salver designed by Sir Edwin Landseer for the Sixth Duke in memory of his brother the Fifth Duke.

ABOVE The Silver and Gold Vaults.
LEFT The Fifth Duke's travelling service together with 18th-century London-made items, displayed in the Silver Vault.

The Parlour and The Grotto

As you leave the vaults you will see a large Estate plan dated 1738, showing the Abbey before its rebuilding by Flitcroft. Notice that Bason Pond was at this time circular, with a railed perimeter walk and a frigate in the centre. In the same area are watercolours of the Abbey by Peter Wagon, whom my mother commissioned many years ago to paint our first home in Suffolk.

The Parlour boasts a beautifully moulded ceiling dating from c.1660, when this room was one of the main living rooms. In the 17th century, and later in the 18th century, it was furnished as a coffee room with shelves of tea and coffee equipage, where guests could be served the beverage of their choice and study the news sheets or periodicals.

ABOVE *The Last Supper* by Giovanni Salvi (Il Sassoferrato).

The Grotto, or folly, was probably built between the late 1620s and 1641. Over the two doors are the coats-of-arms of the Fourth Earl, quartered with his Countess, Katherine Bridges, and the arms of the Earls and Dukes of Bedford.

The Grotto was designed as a loggia where the family could sit and breathe in the fresh, clean Bedfordshire air. In the Italian tradition it faces north, away from the heat and rays of the sun, then (as now) considered harmful.

A fountain once played in the niche where Bacchus stands. A protégé of Inigo Jones, Isaac de Caus, had built a similar room beneath the Banqueting House in Whitehall and almost certainly designed the grotto at Woburn. The work itself is attributed to Nicholas Stone, Master Mason to Charles I from 1632. The stone is carved to resemble seaweed and stalactites, and the walls and ceiling are inlaid with ormer shells from the Channel Islands. The maritime theme is continued in the 19th-century furniture with carved shells and dolphins.

The chairs are fairly delicate in construction, since they were intended merely to offer people a brief rest in the heat of the day. Carved into the wall of one window arch, we discovered some writing, only partly decipherable, but dated 1654.

Bills show the room was glazed in the 1650s; later wire-grilled glass doors were fitted. My mother has replaced these with plate-glass windows, giving the room an open loggia effect.

Grottoes became fashionable in the 19th century, and a 'ruined' folly was built for the Sixth Duke near the Chinese Dairy. The ground outside is known as the Monks' Burial Ground. In the early 1970s, some human bones discovered here were examined at the Institute of Archaeology and found to date from the Middle Ages.

LEFT *The Virgin in Prayer* by Giovanni Salvi (Il Sassoferrato).
FACING PAGE The Grotto.

The Family at Home

Our move into the Abbey in 2002 was every bit as daunting as it has been exciting. The generations before us had achieved so much in renovating the house and striking a delicate balance between it being a family home and an historic house that they were proud to share and enjoy with their visitors. Our challenge is to ensure that the Abbey remains a home that is full of life and laughter and to enjoy it to the full with Alexandra and Henry.

We hope you will enjoy sharing the following selection of more recent photographs taken from our family album.

The Russells and Racing

By The Dowager Duchess of Bedford

My late husband and I registered the name Bloomsbury Stud in 1966, after the area of London owned and built by the Bedford family. The paddocks on the Stud are named after streets in Bloomsbury, so the mares and foals might be turned out in Great Russell Street one day, Covent Garden the next, while the yearlings might graze in Bloomsbury Square or Bedford Way.

The Fifth Duke was the originator of the family's interest in racing. He bred and raced three Derby winners, Skyscraper (1785), Eager (1791) and the only unnamed horse to win the Derby, known as Son of Fidget (1797). The Seventh Duke was also successful; Admiral Rous was employed by him in 1840 and ran his racing and breeding interests for 20 years. It is said of the renowned administrator Admiral Rous that 'he formed the link between the rough and ready racing of the early 19th century and the highly organised sport that we know today'.

In 1975, we bought a mare called Mrs Moss (a bronze life-size statue of her by Philip Blacker stands in front of the house). She turned out to have been an inspired purchase for she was, as one racing pundit described her, 'a legend in her lifetime'.

Mrs Moss had fifteen foals, twelve of whom were winners, including Pushy (winner of the Queen Mary Stakes at Royal Ascot and the Cornwallis Stakes), Precocious (the unbeaten winner of five races, including the Gimcrack, Norfolk, Molecomb and National Stakes) and Jupiter Island (winner of fourteen races, including the Japan Cup, in which he broke the track record and became the first British-bred horse in the world to run one and a half miles in two minutes twenty-five seconds). Although Mrs Moss died in 1991, many of her descendants are here on the Stud. To date, she is the ancestress of 162 individual winners of 418 races all over the world – Australia, New Zealand,

ABOVE Myself, daughter of Pushy and granddaughter of Mrs Moss, next to the bronze statue of Mrs Moss.
BELOW The Bloomsbury stud buildings.

United States of America, Ireland, Italy, France, Germany, Hong Kong and Japan.

When we registered the name Bloomsbury Stud we also re-registered the Bedford Colours – purple and white stripes, black velvet cap with a gold tassel. We were told last year that they are the third oldest colours in the world still being carried by their original owners. Only the Duke of Devonshire's and The Queen's are older.

Our eldest son, Andrew, is a director of Tattersalls, Europe's leading bloodstock auctioneers, and therefore involved in the thoroughbred industry, so now we hope we can emulate the Dukes of the past and breed classic winners from Woburn again.

There are several exciting descendants of Mrs Moss racing and growing up here at Woburn, and in Australia and New Zealand: Rainbow Dancing, Art of Dance, All by Myself, Precedence, Self Centred, Next One and Dancing Attendance.

TOP RIGHT Bay of Islands wins the Foster's Northumberland Plate on 1 July, 2000, the week Andrew and Louise became engaged.
LEFT The Bedford colours of purple and white stripes with the black and gold tasselled cap.
RIGHT Rainbow Dancing winning le Prix Casimir Delamarre at Longchamp in October 2008.

The Thirteenth and Fourteenth Dukes of Bedford

The Thirteenth Duke

RIGHT Ian, Thirteenth Duke of Bedford with Robin (right) and Rudolf. **BELOW** Ian, Thirteenth Duke, is on the left with Robin in front of him and younger brother Rudolf to far right. Lydia is seated in the foreground; her children by her previous marriage are Lorna (next to Robin) and Gavin (lying alongside her). Her son with Ian, Francis, is tucked in at Lorna's feet.

LEFT The Duke takes tea with Violet Carson, who played the notorious 'Coronation Street' character, Ena Sharples.
BELOW Three generations of Dukes: Thirteenth, Fourteenth and Fifteenth in 1963.

ABOVE The Duke at Butlin's Holiday Camp with its founder, Billy Butlin.
LEFT Henrietta and Robin's wedding, 20th June 1961.

The Fourteenth Duke

Every generation likes to leave its positive marks. My grandfather did a brilliant job in putting Woburn on the map as a wonderful house to visit, and in creating the Safari Park and Antiques Centre.

Apart from continuing to build upon his father's successes, I would say that my father's great legacy to Woburn was having the foresight and imagination to create the three outstanding golf courses which we have at the Golf Club. The Marquess' course was named after my father at Alex Hay's suggestion, in recognition of what he had done for the great game of golf.

My father was not only a wonderful father to Robbie, Jamie and me, but also a great friend and mentor to many people both here at Woburn and further afield.

ABOVE Robin and Henry Cecil, Ascot 1980. LEFT Manuel Pinero, Robin and Bernhard Langer in 1981.

BELOW Robin, Henrietta , Andrew and Robbie at Jamie's christening

LEFT Robin with his 'best friend', Charles Downer. BELOW Henrietta and Robin at five years old in London. BOTTOM Robin taking tea in the Great Hall of People in Beijing with the then Vice Premier of the People's Republic of China, Mr Li Peng, on the occasion of the presentation of 22 Milu (Père David) deer in 1985.

LEFT Robin leaning on his favourite sign. ABOVE Robin and Jamie, 1979. RIGHT Robin presents The Dunhill Masters Trophy to Lee Trevino.

RIGHT Robin and Henrietta on their 40th wedding anniversary.

Restoration and Development

Rather like the Forth Bridge, maintaining the fabric of the Abbey is a continual and ongoing process. The fabric is old and all the main edifices are built in a soft, local limestone, Tottenhoe clunch, which needs constant maintenance. This means that we have a phased annual repair programme to keep the exterior in good order. The restoration of Chambers Bridge and the carved tympanum over the East Court were two of the major projects completed in the 1990s.

Chambers Bridge was in very poor condition. As it is also a dam and cascade between two lakes, the repair work was given top priority. Fortunately, the success of the Tina Turner concert in 1990 allowed us to proceed with this work. The stone face was decayed and some of the balustrading had fallen; the faces of the arches and cascade were repaired and the balustrades taken down, repaired and re-fixed.

At around the same time it was discovered that the carved tympanum over the East Court had decayed badly, and there was a danger that pieces of carved stone, some of them weighing nearly a ton, would fall on anyone using the East Court door. This project was assisted by proceeds from the Dire Straits concert (1992). A full-size drawing, 37 x 7 ft (11 x 2m), was made to establish the original details of the Garter Star and Coronet

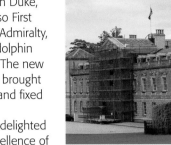

of the Fourth Duke, who was also First Lord of the Admiralty, hence the dolphin supporters. The new carving was brought to Woburn and fixed in position.

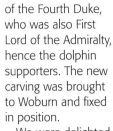

We were delighted that the excellence of craftsmanship in both these projects was acknowledged when the Stone Federation of Great Britain presented its 1993 top award to the architect, Pamela Ward, and the main contractor, J. Bysouth. Further recognition was given in 1995 when Chambers Bridge received a Civic Trust commendation.

Other recent repairs have included work to all the chimneys, the East Court steps and pavings. Renovation of the South and West Fronts of the Abbey is now complete. Work on the central pavilion's north and south-west corners was completed at the end of the 1990s, as was the water-proofing of the south terrace and repairs to the south terrace retaining wall. The South Court roof had to be re-slated and the lead gutters renewed but during this work a major outbreak of dry rot came to light, so that had to be rectified. In 2007 the walls looking on to the courtyard of the South Court were partially renovated.

Slightly less than half of the 40 acre (16 ha) area on which the Abbey complex sits is surrounded by a ha-ha built for the Sixth Duke in the 1830s. Designed so as not to interrupt the landscape viewed from inside the Abbey, parts of the boundary wall were crumbling and no longer capable

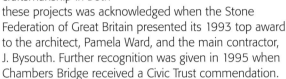

ABOVE Before and after the restoration of Chambers Bridge, completed with income from the Tina Turner concert.
TOP RIGHT The West tympanum during and after restoration.
RIGHT AND BELOW The South front during restoration.

of retaining the ground it was designed to hold in place. This retaining wall was repaired on the south side in 2006–2007 and all the iron fencing refurbished. Additionally, a drain was laid from the ha-ha to the Lower Hop Garden, which in one area had to be sunk down 15 ft (4.5m). The retaining wall around the Chinese Dairy Pond was also crumbling and this was repaired in 2008. The Dairy itself also received attention and some of the woodwork was found in need of repair before repainting. The folly Grotto opposite the Dairy was causing such concern that it had to be closed off to visitors. However, following conservation work by a team from English Heritage, restoration of the Grotto was completed in 2009, enabling visitors to peer into the interior, set with fossils brought up from the West Country. A metal framework has been trained with plants to reconstruct the appearance afforded to Victorian visitors. The road from the town passes Lower Drakelow Pond, where the Temple on the island was completely refurbished. Also in 2008 a new access road was put in place to ease traffic in and out of the complex, while the public entrance and facilities such as the Duchess' Tea Room were given a facelift. A complete modernisation of the fire and security systems within the complex has been carried out. This includes a hard-wired fire alarm system, emergency escape lighting, the installation of lightning conductors and a clip-on fall arrest system around the roof.

A programme of repair and conservation also continues within the Abbey. In 1998 it was decided to restore the very fragile Chinese wallpaper in the Ballroom. This involved initial non-aqueous cleaning of the wallpaper in situ. The border, the decorative laminate and all linings were removed from the walls. In the conservators' studio the wallpaper was separated from the laminate, cleaned and relined. The walls of the room were prepared with a new lining to receive the conserved wallpaper, which was then in-filled and retouched. Care of the collections themselves is continuous and is now much more apparent than in the early days of public opening during the later 1950s, when the Abbey was accessible every day of the year and made removal of objects for conservation or restoration more difficult. In Queen Victoria's Bedroom, the large painting of the trial of William, Lord Russell, by Sir George Hayter, had become so dull that it was difficult to make out the details. It depicts an important event in family history, when the execution of William in 1683 led to the Earls being granted a Dukedom; moreover, following her visit in 1841, Queen Victoria mentioned the painting when describing the bedroom in her journal entry. Hence in 2008 it was decided to bring the painting back to its former glory. Now its bright colours are restored and details, such as the spectators to the trial, stand out much more clearly. A future project is the renovation of the State Bed in the same room.

TOP RIGHT Before and after restoration of the Chinese wallpaper.
ABOVE The Chinese Dairy, during and after restoration.
RIGHT Members of the Curator's team of housekeepers cleaning fire dogs. **FAR RIGHT** Brushing one of the numerous books around the house. **BELOW** The Holland Library during redecoration in 1994.

The Gardens

On his return from the Grand Tour of Europe in 1787, Francis, the Fifth Duke of Bedford, began great improvements to the 42 acres (17 ha) around the Abbey. An indoor tennis court and riding school were built by Henry Holland, but sadly these were pulled down in 1949/50 due to dry rot found in the timbers. He also built the Chinese Dairy and the Orangery, known today as the Sculpture Gallery.

After the death of the Fifth Duke in 1802, his brother, John, carried on his work. His vision was that the Pleasure Grounds should be a garden with fine trees and plants, as well as fine buildings. Humphry Repton was commissioned to help make this vision reality. His ideas were written and illustrated in his 'Red Book' of 1804. Not all of these ideas were completed in the Gardens. Much of his work was carried out in the Deer Park.

The garden today is Victorian in style. It includes a hornbeam maze, a woodland garden, ponds, herbaceous borders and a unique curved greenhouse used for growing camellias. The plan, however, is to introduce some of Repton's original ideas for the garden areas.

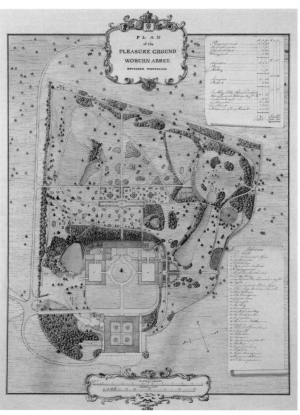

ABOVE 1838 map of the Abbey Gardens at their height in horticulture and used today as a guide on the Abbey Gardens restoration project.

RIGHT View of West Front of the Abbey with Repton in the foreground.

1755
John Bertram supplies John, 4th Duke of Bedford, with plants from America. He later became botanist to King George III

1743
On the birth of his daughter, John, 4th Duke, plants evergreens

1730
The original Kew Gardens are designed

1795
Observations on the Theory and Practice of Landscape Gardening published by Humphry Repton

1787–1789
Sculpture Gallery and Chinese Dairy built

1822–1825
Camellia House and Gothic seat built

1816
Ecological experiment at Woburn is published in the *Hortus Gramineus Woburnensis*

1804
Doric Temple and Grotto built

1844
Francis, 7th Duke, donates entire orchid collection to Queen Victoria, who passes them on to Kew

1838
Rockery constructed

1833
Maze planted

1700	1710	1720	1730	1740	1750	1760	1770	1780	1790	1800	1810	1820	1830	1840	1850

3RD DUKE	4TH DUKE	5TH DUKE	6TH DUKE	7TH DUKE

ABOVE Camellia House seen from the private gardens.
RIGHT The Camellia House.

TOP A view from the Abbey Gardens.
ABOVE The Chinese Dairy.
LEFT The Folly.

1877
Royal Parks and Gardens founded

1914–1918
First World War. Gardeners go to war, abandoning their gardens

1927
First case of Dutch elm disease recorded

1939
Dig for victory during World War II. Lawns are dug up to grow crops

1955
Woburn Abbey opens to the public

2006
First phase of Woburn Gardens Development

1870 1880 1890 1900 1910 1920 1930 1940 1950 1960 1970 1980 1990 2000 2010

H DUKE | 9TH DUKE | 11TH DUKE | 12TH DUKE | 13TH DUKE | 15TH DUKE

10TH DUKE

14TH DUKE

WOBURN
GARDEN TRAIL
Watch us Grow

Welcome to the Gardens. We hope that you will enjoy your time here with us. If you follow the signposts to the Garden Trail Information points, you will be able to find out more about the history of the gardens, the wonderful trees and plants here and our plans to recreate parts of Repton's original vision for the Pleasure Grounds in the future. It is 'work in progress' and we hope that you will come back again and watch us grow. You can enjoy your visit even more by downloading regular podcasts from Martin Towsey, Gardens Manager, from our website www.woburn.co.uk reflecting the changes in season and updates on our progress.

Louise Bedford

Woburn Enterprises

Woburn Enterprises aims to ensure that all our members, guests and visitors enjoy the unique Woburn experience on every visit. We continuously strive to offer quality with a friendly, efficient service and value for money, while generating the revenue needed to help preserve Woburn's unique fabric and treasures and to conserve the many species of animals that we care so much about. This is not only for the benefit of future generations of the Russell family, but also for those who live and work with such dedication at Woburn. The businesses operating under the enterprise umbrella are:

Woburn Abbey houses the famous family collection of art and antiques; the adjacent Sculpture Gallery offers a stunning venue for weddings and functions and the Antique Centre is stocked with a myriad of constantly changing items for sale, all within the enclosed Deer Park, home to nine species of deer roaming freely within the grounds.

Woburn Golf Club is set in outstanding countryside, with three of the best British championship courses and has hosted many major tournaments over the years.

Woburn Safari Park is the national award-winning centre of conservation and education, home to over 70 species of animals, 26 of which are currently breeding programmes, and built on 320 acres (130 ha) of parkland to allow the animals freedom to roam.

And, **The Inn at Woburn,** located at the heart of Woburn village, offers a warm and friendly welcome to visitors also able to enjoy their award-winning restaurant, Olivier's.

We would like to thank you for helping make Woburn what it is today – a living attraction for all ages.

Events at Woburn

With its unique setting, Woburn Abbey presents a stunning backdrop to many exciting and varied events.

We have hosted concerts and performances from such stars as Neil Diamond, Tina Turner, Dire Straits, Elton John, Michael Ball, Van Morrison, Curtis Stigers, Ronnie Scott's Big Band, Julian Lloyd Webber and Hayley Westenra; Shakespeare plays under summer skies in the Abbey Gardens; magical opera and ballet performances in the Sculpture Gallery; craft fairs; art exhibitions and charity events; vintage car rallies; championship golf tournaments; themed dining and animal conservation fundraising events.

Our website www.woburn.co.uk carries constantly updated event listings.